Crooked Letter.

Mary Beth Davis

Made with ❤ on the BookLeaf Publishing Platform
www.bookleafpub.in
www.bookleafpub.com

Dedication

*To Mary and Jason Davis —
I told you I'd get around to it
eventually.*

Preface

I give you the mausoleum of all hope and desire…I give it
to you not that you may remember time, but that you
might forget it now and then for a moment and not spend
all of your breath trying to conquer it.
—William Faulkner, *The Sound and the Fury*

*M-I-Crooked Letter-Crooked Letter-I-Crooked Letter -
Crooked Letter-I-Humpback-Humpback-I*

Acknowledgements

Writing a chapbook has always been a dream of mine, and I owe so many my undying gratitude and abounding love. Thank you, Bookleaf Publishing, for this journey's joy. <u>Mama and Daddy:</u> Thank you for constantly reminding me I'm a writer. <u>Laura</u>: Thank you for being my rock. You know how much you matter to me. <u>Jon</u>: Thank you for your unwavering support and unending well of goofs and gags. <u>Hannah</u>: Thank you for being my biggest fan. Your encouragement saw me through some of the blackest days. <u>Devon</u>: Thank you for letting me write when I should've been doing the dishes. <u>Mary Lane</u>: You are my heart. Thank you for all the free editing and for teaching me the importance of using "lie" correctly. <u>Jo</u>: I probably won't be taking you to Paris anytime soon, but we're one step closer! <u>Lindsey</u>: We're finally off to the races! You're up next. Finally, thank you to <u>Eudora Welty and William Faulkner</u>. (Will, you may not have actually said that quote about understanding the world vis-a-vis Mississippi, but I don't doubt you would have agreed with it.) Your lanterns lit my way.

Once Upon A Time

There was a kingdom of cotton and cornfields, and there
was sweet olive and magnolias and gardenias,
and there were bobcats and horses and cows, and people
who lived in mansions and in shacks with tin roofs
and steep potholes that collected the rain like green well
water, and there was a girl who was growing up, but she
didn't know it,and there was love and what she thought
was love, so there was heartache, too, and there were
mockingbirds and blue jays and doves and there were
sharks' teeth in creek beds, gleaming slick and there
wasn't a lot of time or money but there were plenty of
stories and this is one of them.

Crooked Letter.

Tell me a story – the screen door bangs. A rusted nail has held it shut
for the last thirty years, and they'd change the nail before they'd change the door. Behind us, there's the garden overflowing with things like sunflowers and corn, but they keep the tomatoes and cucumbers in the very back so thieves can't easily get to them, which means we can't easily get to them either, but we still try because nothing tastes better than sweet, fresh sunlight and promises soaked in God's tears and you can run on holy ground if your feet are bare and your toes are muddy, and
you laugh you laugh you laugh –

Tell me a story - the screen door bangs. It has holes in it now that weren't there last time, but we've learned to keep quiet. Behind us, there's the garden that's nothing but churned, dried mounds but
we still believe that there will be food again when spring is back, and summer is back, and the cold isn't permanent or reminding us that we are composed of water and ribcages and cool breaths and mornings where we try to forget the bumps we heard in the night so instead we think about how hope feels like a cannonball

into a pool, all light and bathwater, and we could run if
we wanted to if our feet were in the right socks and
boots,but we don't we don't we don't –

Tell me a story – instead of a screen door, I have a sliding
one. It glides open smoothly and I go out on the balcony
sometimes to water the herbs in their little plastic pots
andI pretend even though I know we haven't been a 'we'
in a long time, but I try to call every few weeks to give
the illusion that we still could be and to remember the
running that made us feel like we were composed of the
best impossibilities, that we were music, loosed arrows,
blueberrystained lost boys and not victims of another
generation's demons. I pretend we ran because we could,
not to escape the inevitable haunting –

I brush my hand against some sage,
squeeze it in my palm, because
it's the crushing that produces its soil-like scent.
I think about wiping it away but
I can't I can't I can't.

Mud Pie.

It'd bake under the sunshine the way
we used to by the pool on July afternoons,
all wet and sticky and imperfect and
I remember it olfactorily:
chlorine, dirt, grass, suntan lotion, bubblegum, sweat.
Rococo-style water hoses languidly draped across the
yard,
a fan of water spraying upwards,
smoke from the grill curling like diaphanous ribbons —
It was all a declaration.

I can't remember the last time I was willing
to see mud as a blessing,
as a baptism.

It's all Gunpowder.

If a firework explodes outside your house,
but you're not there to see it,
does it become a gunshot?
An angry ache that ricochets off the cold night,
stars becoming buckshot?

Or does it stay a mystery?
A guessing game you play, where if you close
your eyes tight enough you can almost imagine
that you're in a theme park,
that you have paid to witness this extravaganza
instead of being forced to endure it.
You've been a spectator for so long now.

Turns out, you've always been drawn to wonder.
And you've learned that in the end,
it's all gunpowder and smoke and
silence.

*When was the last time you heard a bang and didn't
think of a body?*

Polite Dinner Conversation.

You notice they keep plants in their living room.
Parlor palms and peperomia –
they are meant to make the space seem fresh;
to bring life into an otherwise manufactured
environment.

Maybe they notice the creekbed in your walk or the
cotton in your spine
because they ask you if you ever gardened before you
came to the city.
Asked you if you had ever tried to keep a thing alive
before.

You tell them no, not really –
but your father planted tomatoes and cucumbers and
sunflowers,
and sweet olive and gardenias and wisteria,
and to this day the taste or smell of it all reminds you of
sunlight.

They smile politely and sip their chardonnay.

Girl Talk.

Are you going out like that?
You need to put on a little color,
maybe some mascara at least.
Remember to suck in your gut when you walk
and press your tongue to the roof
of your mouth — no, really, see
the difference it makes?
Oh, and don't wear that — it's too short
too lowcut
too tempting
too much.
You don't want to be the reason your
brothers in Christ sin, do you?
Well?
Do you?

Young and Dumb.

I drink beer in college
because I think it'll make me seem
like the kind of woman a man
can trust.

I walk down
Beale Street, sucking
a weeping green bottle and
hoping a man notices how
relaxed and fun and easygoing
I am.

But I don't like beer as much
as I like attention so
I just pretend to drink,
and I've been pretending
ever since.

Marriage.

We do not dance in the glow of the purring refrigerator's
light.
We do not kiss at stoplights or in grocery store aisles,
and we do not sing to each other with our eyes in such a
way that others envy our symphony.

Our love is common in the clearest way:
I will fold your pants if you wipe off the counters,
We will alternate who does the dishes, and argue over
who gets the remote.
I'll complain about your driving, and you'll complain
about mine.
I will steal your t-shirts, and you will steal my
conditioner.
We will have too much sex, and then not nearly enough,
and sometimes we won't even notice when the other
crawls into bed with a bonetiredness --
 a crumpled bag or wrung out rag, I mean to say that
you crawl into bed, and even though I'm unaware of you
in that moment,
we both know you can't go anywhere else, and this is
safety in its most pure way.

There are no grand romantic gestures, unless you count

picking up pizza for dinner
 or opening a bottle of cheap wine on a Friday afternoon
as being romantic,
which I do, because romance doesn't mean "things" it
just means "you."

This is not the love that will make the big-screen, or
inspire tragedies.
This love is steady, comfortable
woolen, knit socks, not sheer red lace,
and it's everything we've been wanting.

It is the love that we need,
the love that lasts,
the love that stays,
we hope.

What My Mother Taught Me.

I wear my mother's blanket like a coat of armor,
the yarn crocheted together into millions of
soft fingers that embrace me with the
gentle reminder that I am safest when
I rest in tenderness.

The colors I hand picked when
I was young and knew the world. Now,
I am still young, but the kind of young
that knows the only thing I can be certain of is that
if I want to save anyone,
I must look at them through the lens of
kaleidoscopekindness, knowing and seeing them
one stitch at a time.

This is grace.

Collapsing.

I fall beneath the breaking of things,
existing in the cracks, this splinter of space,
and wonder how long I can make it in the
everything and nothing that coincides here.

That which brushes against me like an oily black cat,
 rubs against the fragile ache within me,
purring to be seen and demanding to be felt.

I tell it no, but the truth is
I got use to the claws
a long time ago.

Smoke.

Do you want to meet me in the kitchen for a smoke?
Because I want us to talk about whether or not
happiness is a sustainable thing
as we try to negotiate all the ways we can love and hurt
each other
in a single season.
If you're too busy, I'll say I understand,
which I guess means that I'll still smile at you when you
crack a joke, and
I'll still fold your shirts, and make the bed with hospital-
like care,
with patience, with the coppery tang of bitterness on my
tongue.

So don't mind me: I'll just be sitting here waiting,
smoking,
watching the couple in the wrinkled t-shirts walking
handnhand outside our window,
and I'll wonder how love just happened to them like
that,
and how they managed to keep it.

Golden Days.

There were golden days,
where September suspended in amber,
meant the beginning of the return to routine.

There were golden days,
where rituals patinated and known,
meant a honeyed homecoming.

There were golden days,
Where we knew what safety was and that it
meant comfort had a soul and a pair of blue eyes.

There were golden days,
Where seeing you again meant everything,
felt like goldfinch wings fluttering,
meant that the sand finally stopped its falling.

There were golden days,
and then they were gone

we don't know who we are
if we are no longer the special boys and girls
of the golden days.

Not All Cages Come With Bars.

A prisoner sits in a gilded cage,
surrounded by comforts both plush and luxurious.
She wants for nothing, but still wonders
what the difference between a cell and a home are,
when you lack the power necessary,
to free yourself.

Sacrifice.

I used to think sacrifice was death,
the ultimate loss given to preserve another's life,
but now I know that sacrifice is really all the little ways
I tried to save you to the detriment of myself.

Loneliness.

Loneliness is not the state of being alone,
but the knowledge that you are not
understood by those whose
approval you crave the most.

Happy Ending.

maybe no one's love is shiny, high gloss
resolution, slick as an opal sheen, pearlescent pink,
radiant and 1940s lipstick red. maybe your love fell off
the shelf, too. maybe you've been pricking your way
through brittle glass and piercing fragments for far too
long and your fingertips are stained purple-blue, crow
tipped and tar-like. maybe on the good days, when the
clean-up doesn't feel like slogging through blue water
pregnant with ice and all your best intentions, maybe
then the love will feel worth it and not like a death
sentence you never saw coming. Or maybe the question
will always flit through your mind, jade like
hummingbird wings, impressed with longing and a little
snark: how do you end happy, anyway?

Grief Museum.

If grief belonged in a museum, I'd study it like God.

Take out a magnifying glass and peer in, take gentle,
slow steps around it to analyze and assess it from all
angles in all kinds of light. I'd buy tickets for the
privilege, ignore the other mourners, use a bench as my
pew, focus on the depth of it all, that cavernous
darkness, that sacred maw, that hollow curving shell that
yearns to listen for an answer or a reason or an
explanation. I'd see how it gives and how it takes away.

Witness me, I'd cry. *Look at my hands, see this pierced
heart. There was once a time when I wouldn't have been
able to name you, but now I look at you and see all the
best of me stuck here behind you, flattened against the
cold marble while you grin, masticating, teeth gleaming
and winking like stars, nictitating behind this
fingerprinted glass.*

But I don't speak. I ignore the weight of it,
this heavy sorrow, because I'm 28 and a perfectionist
people pleaser, which means the only thing I know how
to really study is everyone's grief but my own.

Recovering People Pleaser.

Your bitterness over my being used to be a bruise I wore casually.

A harsh word.
A cracked teacup.
A cold stare.
A smashed plate.

But now you can no longer keep me in a bottle on the shelf, tucked behind all the others you've deemed unsafe, unworthy, unlovable, unwanted, unneeded, unmoored.

I am not a hideable thing; I do not go quietly into the dark night.
I cannot hold your hatred in my starcrossed palms, and internalize it so that your poison becomes my problem.

Light does not have time to worry over what the darkness thinks of it.

Older But Wiser.

I drink whiskey now because
I don't go to Beale Street, anymore.
And if you asked me to describe myself,
"easygoing" and "fun"
wouldn't even make it in the top five but

I trust myself,
and I can say with confidence that I am
neither origami nor court jester;
there's no manic pixie dream, here.

I mean, I still care what you think —
but I'm a lot less concerned with it
than I used to be.

So, instead of wondering
if you'll like me, I've started wondering
if I'll even like you.

Hunting.

As a child,
my father takes me hunting
on a haunted morning,
mist moving like ghosts across the still field.
The doe is small, the shot is sure,
but I am convinced she is still breathing,
convinced that she would have let us pet her,
She let us get so close! after all.
We gut her at my grandfather's,
and I marvel at how I didn't know how red the wild was,
and how brave I am for seeing it.
So I go and wander, singing showtunes under my breath,
thinking about the way it all works, life I guess, and I
wade through
the leaves like spilled pennies, and I
kick the base of an oak tree with my
cornflower tennis shoe —
    We are led to those who help us most to grow.
There's a mockingbird watching me.
If I can just reach out...

The End.

On the interstate between here and Alabama,
there's a wooden sign nailed to an old tree,
and it says, "Jesus Save Me" and even with
thirty years of experience, I still haven't learned
how to pray it any better.

9 789369 543830